The Charmer

Life of Serial Killer George Waterfield Russell Jr

Jack Smith

Efforts have been made to ensure that the information in this book is accurate and complete. However, the author and the publisher do not warrant the accuracy of the information, text, and graphics contained within the book due to the rapidly changing nature of science, research, known and unknown facts, and the internet. The author and the publisher do not hold any responsibility for errors, omissions, or contrary interpretation of the subject matter herein. This book is presented solely for motivational and informational purposes only.

Warning
Throughout the book, there are some descriptions of murders and crime scenes that some people might find disturbing. There might be also some language used by people involved in the murders that may not be appropriate.

Note
Words in italic are quoted words from verbatim and have been reproduced as is, including any grammatical errors and misspelled words.

ISBN 9798877046023

Printed in the United States

Contents

George, the Goody Two Shoes

As terrible as the lives of some criminals might end up being, most began with just as much promise and expectation as anyone else's. Contrary to some narrowminded beliefs, the criminals who perpetrate some of the worst crimes (which captivate endless cycles in the news media), are not usually hatched out of some monster factory, but typically got their start in life as, well, fairly ordinary individuals.

And much the same can be said of George Russell Jr. In fact, he was well liked in the local community in which he grew up. Known as The Charmer, he was by no means viewed as a perfect kid, and had even had a few scrapes with law enforcement in his youth—but even the cops that had some limited dealings with him as a minor, were always impressed with how "smart" and "nice" the youngster seemed to be.

In fact, one cop on the beat by the name of Glendon Booth would later report, "The first time I saw Georgie, he was in trouble for some petty thing, maybe truancy, and the Youth Bureau had given him some work around the station. He was 13 or 14, a little bitty kid, well dressed, frail, innocent, very likeable. He could charm your socks off. He was the last kid on Mercer Island you'd expect to turn into our biggest nightmare."

"Georgie" in fact, seemed to have an ambition to become a cop himself. He was still an adolescent when he befriended the local police enough to become an informant. He was soon a regular face at the station tipping the police off to a wide variety of petty theft and mischief that his peers were engaged in.

Of course, young people don't tend to look to kindly on those deemed to be a "snitch" and not everyone looked favorably on George's after school activities at the local police department. They thought that he was a bit too much of a "goody two shoes" for their tastes. Little did anyone know, however, rather than being a goody goody—George Russell would end up shocking the world with his crimes.

The Early Days

George Russell Jr. was born to his mother and father Joyce and George Russell Sr., back in 1958, when the child's parents lived in Florida. The parents' union was not a happy one however, and George's father (and namesake) decided to part company. It was after his parents went their separate ways that his mom ended up taking her son up to the Northwest, all the way to Mercer Island, in the state of Washington.

His mother had moved to take up with her new boyfriend and soon fiancé—Dr. Mobley—a local dentist. Joyce and Dr. Wonzel Mobley would soon have a child of their own between them, little baby Erika. George would frequently be tasked with babysitting his new half-sister—a task that he would later complain about, yet at the time, he took it as a kind of badge of honor.

He initially took the responsibility quite seriously and would frequently cancel hanging out with his own friends just to take care of his little sister. But as much as he wanted to be the responsible little brother, it wasn't long before he was out of the house roaming the streets. He would often take his dog on long walks through the neighborhood well after the sun went down.

It was on one of these long walks that George first caught the attention of police. He was spotted by a patrolman who just wondered what he was doing out so late. The officer struck up a conversation and was impressed with how mature the kid acted—almost like a little adult. He was sure to tell the youngster to run on home, but the impression was made.

Police would later encounter George again, and through further dialogue, they actually agreed to let him volunteer at the station. George seemed to leap at the chance, and the police believed that this kind of hands-on mentorship might be just what the youth needed. Soon George was a regular, enthusiastic face at the station.

He was there at least twice a week, and helped with odd jobs around the precinct, such as taking out trash, cleaning, and replenishing office supplies. On occasion, he was even allowed to answer the phone, the police were apparently tickled to death to have this kid answer the line, in his prepubescent voice, declaring that it was the "Mercer Island Police" to whom the caller was speaking.

Although he wasn't paid for his efforts, he was often rewarded with (junk) food and soft drinks. Soon enough, George was telling everyone he knew that he wanted to be a police officer when he grew up. He became really close with the police down at the station in the meantime. So close, they would often tell him their own problems and struggles in life.

Interestingly however, they would soon come to realize, that as much as they were opening up to their young protégé, he was divulging next to nothing about himself. They would try to make inquiries into his personal life, but beyond him saying that his step-dad was a dentist, and his mother a teacher—his personal family life always seemed to draw a complete blank.

Soon his buddies at the station realized how uncomfortable he was in talking about family life, they simply gave up trying. They didn't realize that the boy was trying to substitute the family he felt so ill at ease with, with the brotherly love he experienced down at the police station. They were just thankful for his help—and as things progressed, they were also thankful for his *tips.*

For it was shortly into their relationship with each other, that George began to feed the station all kinds of tips about what his peers were up to on Mercer Island. George was only around 13 at the time, but the middle-school kids he ran with were already committing all kinds of criminal mischief. One of the most brazen incidents involved George's close friend, Boris Brocket.

Boris and a couple of other kids they knew, had broken into a local music store and stolen a whole truckload of guitars. The instruments were then stashed at Boris' house. A short time after the heist, Boris invited George over and showed him the loot. Rather than being excited at the take, George quickly chided his friend, telling him he shouldn't have done it.

The next thing Boris knew, the police were knocking on his parents' door. The cops knew what he did and demanded he hand over the instruments. Ultimately after the equipment was returned, Boris got off with just a lecture. He was likely lucky to get off with just a simple warning.

The whole incident unfolded as it did of course, courtesy of George the informant. And George wasn't done yet, for a short time later he tipped off the police about a bike-stealing ring, gaining even further appreciation from the Mercer Island cops. They paid George back by letting him become more involved in official police business.

He was even allowed to tag along in the patrol car. George was now like an honorary member of the force, and it's said that he even had a little notepad with him, in which he prodigiously took notes about all that he saw and heard. George wanted to be a cop, and he seemed to be willing to work *hard* enough to make that happen.

But George himself was not immune to getting into adolescent mischief. As was the case in May of 1973, when he was 15 years old. For it was shortly after his 15th birthday that George and a couple of friends decided to run off to the nearby town of Cle Elum. These underage kids were playing hooky, big time, and basically running away from home.

Law enforcement eventually got a hold of them, and they were forced to explain themselves to the cops. George had a story prepared, claiming that they were all on a "ski trip" sponsored by North Mercer Middle School. They said that they simply lost interest in the trip and fell away from the rest of the group.

It was a fairly good excuse, since it was plausible enough to be believed, and yet was very hard for this beat cop to be able to verify on the spot. For all he knew, the kid was telling the truth. He did however, insist on double-checking with the kids' parents, before he gave the all clear. George had already prepared for this event as well. He knew his parents wouldn't be home, so it wouldn't matter if the police called—or not.

He also knew that the parents of one of the guys he was with, would be gone as well. It was only the one other friend of the group whose folks might have actually been home at the time. For him, he had prepared for this contingency in advance. Knowing that they might be stopped, questioned, and have their home numbers called, he had instructed this kid to give out the number to a local payphone if asked.

The kid however, not as cool under pressure as George, panicked and, despite himself, ended up giving his *actual* home number. This was the key that unraveled the whole plot. For no sooner than that cop rang up this number, he heard the confusion of a parent on the other end, insisting that *no such field trip* had ever been planned. It was now clear that these kids were skipping school.

Now that George had been caught breaking the rules however, his reasoning for doing what he did left the authorities quite confused. Instead of just admitting that he was out for some kicks, when asked why he had run off to Cle Elum, George came up with a very strange rationale. He stated that he had "heard" that the police back in Mercer Island were trying to "frame" him for a "burglary."

Yes, once he was in trouble, he not only made up wild excuses, but in his process of assigning imagined blame, he also didn't hesitate to throw his good friends of the Mercer Island Police Department, under the bus.

This sort of behavior would become a lifelong pattern for George Russell Jr.

The Start of His Criminal Career

George Russell Jr. started high school in the Fall of 1973. Even though his birthday from the previous May made him a little older than his classmates, he was so small that his edge in age was immediately negated by his scrawny, short frame. Nevertheless, he was funny, congenial, and had a winning smile. He soon became quite popular with his peers.

George in fact, began to run with the more popular kids at his high school, regularly hanging out with all of the preps and jocks on campus. George was typically viewed as the street-smart kid among the bunch, and although he was always warm and friendly to those in his social circles, he would offer a window into another world. For that preppie, popular kid that wanted to delve into drugs or even a brush with the law, it was George that would provide glimpses of such things.

George, for example, managed to sneak a whole gang of his friends into a Led Zeppelin concert by way of sheer street smarts alone. George had gotten his hands on a regular old parking attendant uniform and used the getup to gain access to the employees' entrance. He then connived to allow his buddies right in with him.

All was not right in George's family home however, and soon his parents would head for divorce. It seems that his dentist stepfather had found love in the arms of another woman, and his mother in the meantime, had been given a promotion and teaching gig thousands of miles away.

She took the gig just as much to get away from the drama of her personal life, as she did to move up in the world. She took little Erika with her in the meantime, even while foisting her son off on his reluctant stepdad. Stepdad Wonzel in the meantime, had married his lover, a girl 12 years younger than him, named Kris.

George, like many of his friends who paid a visit, was rather smitten with the attractive young woman. It wouldn't be long however, before this puppy dog infatuation took on a more sinister caste. Something that Kris herself would never forget.

Trifling and troubling George in the meantime, had managed to get on the bad side of many of his peers, by not only becoming a narc, but by also regularly divulging confidential info he found in the police records down at the station. Some kids complained about what was happening, and word got back to the precinct.

Leaks like this were not tolerated, and once the source of the leaked info was traced back to George, he was told not to return to the station. George was devastated by this rejection, and it would not only see him give up on a future career in law enforcement, it would send him on an entire new trajectory—as far outside the law as one could possibly get.

George's stepdad Wonzel in the meantime, seems to have been a pretty patient and generous guy, considering how he took in his stepson George, even after divorcing his stepson's mother. Many guys likely would have figured such things were no longer their responsibility. George wasn't even his biological offspring—why should he foot the bill for George's real mother and father? Most people likely would have shrugged off any notion of such a thing.

Nevertheless, the long-suffering of stepdad Wonzel seems to have finally worn thin by the time George reached his senior year of high school. Unable to handle Goerge's behavior, Wonzel ended up pawning him off on an old dental college friend, a certain Dr. Michael Washington. This meant a slight relocation off Mercer Island, and George transferred schools to Inglemoor High School.

Dr. Washington, in the meantime, was a no-nonsense authoritarian figure who tried to instill discipline and order into George's otherwise chaotic life. Washington had George up early in the morning doing chores before school, and kept him up late at night studying for his classes. Mr. Washington thought that he just might be the one who was stern enough to whip George into shape—but he would turn out *wrong* on all counts.

It wasn't long before George, unable to handle the strict and stern regimen, began to rebel. He began hanging out with a bunch of other rebellious youngsters and soon he was having run-ins with the law over a whole string of minor offenses. It was shortly after he turned 18, that one bust in particular put him in jail.

The sentence was just a couple of days in County Jail, but as soon as he was out, he was back at it. This led to a few more days in the slammer. Shortly thereafter, he trespassed again, and the next thing he knew he was booked for a whole month behind bars. This would become a familiar theme during his late teens and early 20s, but nevertheless, he always managed to weasel his way out of anything more serious than misdemeanor charges and light sentences.

In typical George fashion he was friendly with both the judge and the arresting officers. In one particular incident in particular, this close relationship was rather telling. George had been prowling around on the second floor of a construction site, when he was caught by one of his old pals down at the precinct— Manny Rucker.

The officer when trying to apprehend him, actually fell and got hurt. George apparently attempted to show some concern. And at the station, when encountering the officer, he made a point to ask him how he was doing. The officer responded that he was fine, and asked Geroge why he was so worried about his condition.

George is said to have replied, "Man, anytime you get caught for something and a cop gets hurt, they charge your ass for assault!" It was only then that the true reason behind his concern came out. He wasn't so much worried about the officer's health, as he was about his own skin.

Really, George was only worried he would get hit up with additional charges. A fear that Officer Manny

Rucker relieved, by assuring the young man that he wouldn't blame him for the fall, since he considered it his own fault that he fell. It was likely a kind courtesy on the part of Officer Rucker. For it was due to this last-minute bit of generosity on Officer Rucker's part, that George was simply nailed for criminal trespass, rather than anything more substantial.

But these criminal trespasses would continue, and although all of the things he stole equated to petty crime, George seemed to get a thrill from sneaking into the homes of others. In retrospect this was clearly the beginning of George Russell Jr. becoming a predator.

Initially he was only breaking into homes to snatch a few petty items. Soon enough however, he would be snatching people.

On The Mercer Island Beat

George continued to be a strange enigma as he lurked around like a petty thieving vagabond on Mercer Island. By his early 20s he was something of a local legend. All small, closeknit communities seem to have them—that strange local guy, who sits at a coffee shop all hours of the day, or stands on the street corner, or is permanently plastered in the back of a bus, muttering and rambling to anyone who would care to listen.

These types are often mocked, ridiculed, and shunned in equal measure by the surrounding community. They are indeed notorious, but they aren't exactly the kind of folks one would invite to a party. But as odd as George had become, he was still well liked. Well liked enough, that acquaintances let him sleep in house boats, or even occasionally let him have the run of a whole vacation house.

Washington's Mercer Island was a rich enclave and although George was now basically a homeless man, he still carried himself as if he were among the elite. Even if he was homeless, he still made sure he wore the best designer (even if they were stolen) threads, and spoke as if he were someone important. He was also still in quite good with the police—which was rather bizarre, since he was being arrested by them during most of their encounters.

Even so, jail became almost like a second home to him, where he got free meals, a warm room, and access to cable TV. George was certainly troubled, and the police obviously knew that, but he was still as friendly and congenial as ever. Even behind bars, he conversed with his police pals, cracked jokes, and traded favors.

During his jail stints, he was often rewarded with gigs such as being made an attendant at the commissary. The commissary is a makeshift shop in a prison, where inmates can use the little bit of money they earn from prison work, to buy soda, candy, and snacks. It might seem silly for grown men to care about getting a junk food fix, but in prison where they are deprived of most luxuries, something as simple as getting a candy bar *is* a big deal.

George was trusted and liked well enough by those in charge of the prison, for him to be placed right at the heart of this time-honored, prison tradition. His arrests for petty theft almost became a joke in themselves, with George being busted without incident. He usually knew the arresting officers, and George went willingly, with a shrug that said "Alright—you got me!"

Typical, joke-telling George, usually had the whole squad car laughing by the time they rolled up to the police station. The truth was, George got along a whole lot better with the police and prison guards, than he ever did with the inmates. Many of these tough and hardened criminals looked at George with absolute contempt. Especially those who grew up in the poorer surrounding communities.

They typically listened once to George's refined accent and mode of speaking and made the snap judgment that he was not "one of them." This led to many of his fellow inmates hurling terrible insults and slurs in his direction as he was derided as nothing more than a token "pet" of the police. The taunts certainly bothered George, but that didn't stop him from befriending cops.

On the contrary, despite all he had been through—*he still wanted to be a cop.* In between his stints in jail in fact, he occasionally impersonated one himself. He sometimes wore a police hat, and carried a badge to clubs, and claimed to be a "special agent." These claims would get him into a whole lot of mischief when he tried to play cop and get people kicked out of bars.

George exhibited this same mentality when a friend tried to help him out, by getting him a gig as "Assistant Manager" at a local club called, "Tonite's the Nite." He would manage to retain employment at this joint for over two years—but not without incident. He in fact, became quite notorious. He would often let his buddies cut in line, and if anyone questioned his actions, he was quick to chew them out.

He also ran a long-running scam of taking tickets from customers and then reselling them. It wouldn't last forever however, and soon his hijinks caught up with him enough that he was fired from the club.

This latest failure enraged George more than anything else he had failed at. But he didn't blame himself for the ouster—oh no—he blamed those who dared to hold him accountable for his own actions.

And soon he was plotting to wreak vengeance on the club boss, David Israel. He knew that David kept cash in his car and attempted to break into his parked vehicle one night in order to get it.

The cops were called however, and George was put back in jail. He didn't stay there long though, since he literally found a way to weasel his way out. He climbed through a busted overhead window and disappeared.

Police were shocked and dismayed that he was able to slip from their grasp so easily and they began searching the whole area for him. The days continued to wear on however, with George continually giving them the slip. It almost became a joke, since frequent reports of George showing up in various places would come forth—yet he would always be long gone by the time the police arrived on the scene.

Even after a $500 reward was posted, George still managed to elude capture. Folks that knew him even began to report that George would briefly pop up, crack jokes about how no one could catch him, and would then disappear.

The situation was becoming absolutely ridiculous. Finally, the police had enough, and held a stakeout near one of George's most frequent haunts.

They waited and waited, until like some local, mythical beast, the hunted and hounded George Russell Jr. suddenly emerged from the nearby woods. They let him get right out into the open before they pounced. By the time George realized he was being ambushed, it was too late. Knowing he couldn't get away, he fell down crying and screaming, begging the cops to go easy on him.

The police, despite the adrenaline rush, refrained from being overly aggressive, got George in cuffs and put him in the back of a squad car. This time around he was charged with a felony for his prison break, and given a total of 10 months in jail. Some wondered if this stint in prison might somehow reform George, and make him a changed man. But it didn't.

As soon as he was out, he went right back to his devious ways. Throughout much of the rest of his 20s, George roamed the streets like a crooked vagabond, always seeking his next cheat, steal, or con. Interestingly, he also kept in contact with some of his arresting officers.

Not only that, he began to work for them. Falling back on his old pastime of being an informant, he began to narc out his buddies if the police offered him enough incentive to do so. He dropped tips in order to avoid charges on infractions, or to get other perks and privileges.

George at this point had lost a lot of his old friends that he used to run with. Typically, one of three things had transpired. They were either dead, in jail, or had simply grown up from their previous juvenile delinquency, and moved on with their life.

Yes, when many of his peers were finally growing up, getting married, and working full time jobs. George however, like some juvenile delinquent version of Peter Pan was still staying up all night, and getting into trouble. Since his old crew had largely moved on,

George began to focus on a new generation of young people that had cropped up on Mercer Island.

Even more troubling, he began to focus on younger girls in the area. Considering as much, one could speculate that George had some sort of compulsion for these younger minded souls. But his evolution of predation was likely more out of necessity than anything else. Since he had no job, and basically no prospects, he wasn't too appealing to girls his own age, in the 20s.

Yet, he was still able to turn on the charm and impress gullible teenage girls still in high school. One of those girls was Laura Green, who George had met through a mutual friend. Soon George and Laura were hanging out a lot and, despite their age gap, became intimately involved with each other.

So intimate in fact, that George managed to get his underage girlfriend pregnant. They didn't find out until George was behind bars for his latest offense. Both however, came to the conclusion that they weren't ready for parenthood. As such, George's young girlfriend soon found herself within the walls of a local *planned parenthood,* and underwent an abortion.

Incredibly, this incident brought on one of the very rare shows of actual remorse on George's part. George, who had apparently previously insisted that they could have unprotected sexual contact without any repercussions, now took responsibility for what had happened.

Or as George put it in a letter he wrote from prison, "The mistake I apologize for the most—was my inability to provide the proper safeguards that would have prevented the situation that occurred a couple of months ago. I am very, very sorry to have put you through that. And without me being by your side no less. I pray you will forgive me. That was my fault."

Yes, George after multiple stints in jail, in which he blamed everything from the cops, the person he robbed, or the system itself—was now finally taking the blame for something. It was indeed a rare moment, and it would soon pass. Laura would soon come to realize in the meantime, that perhaps being involved with someone twice her age, who was a jailbird, was not the best thing for her.

And after George's six-month term in the slammer came to an end in May of 1987, she was determined to end their relationship. As soon as he came to visit her, she became standoffish, and withdrawn, and although she didn't vocalize her wish to terminate their relationship, Goerge was certainly perceptive enough to catch her drift.

He soon stopped coming around, but not before one final, strange encounter. George's stepdad and stepmom had apparently left town on vacation. The now 29-year-old George took this opportunity to sneak back into his old home and throw an impromptu party.

He promptly invited Laura and tried to make some moves. According to her, he got her alone at one point and attempted to "go down on her." She flatly rejected him however, and it was over. If George was upset, he didn't let on. According to Laura he just shrugged, smiled, and wished her well. But as it pertained to

George and his pent-up animosity—no one ever knew just how angry he really was.

And like many male killers, George had some pretty complex feelings in regard to the female gender. On the one hand, he seemed to genuinely enjoy the company of women, besides the obvious physical gratification he got from them.

He seemed to actually enjoy having long, deep conversations with his female friends. Laura would later find herself amazed thinking of how there were times that they would stay up all night talking about everything under the sun, and how George seemed to be sincerely interested in what she was saying.

Even high school gossip, about which boys were cute, and which were not—was somehow of great interest to George. Yet, at the same time, as friendly and as congenial as George could be with females, he also harbored a deep streak of hidden resentment. Hidden is indeed the correct word to describe it, for there was a lot of animosity that George had long kept under wraps and much of it was centered around the woman who should have been the number one female in his life—*his mother.*

His mom had moved away and left him with his stepdad and his new wife, when he was still an impressionable young teen. In some ways it almost seemed as if she had abandoned him, as if he was unwanted by the very woman who gave birth to him. Such sentiment would be quite clear to those who later examined his life, but George himself would always insist quite the opposite.

He was always quick to tell folks that he decided to stay in Mercer Island all of his own volition. He insisted that it was his choice. He spoke highly of his mother and bragged about the nice house she had back in Maryland, and the big fat salary she made as a college professor. Yet, his friends would later discover that as much as he talked highly about his mom, he never ever visited her.

One friend who went to a get-together at George's stepdad Wonzel's place, would even recall an incident in which George was "tricked" into getting on the phone with his mom. He apparently didn't know it was her, and as soon as he realized as much, he immediately ended the conversation—as if he didn't want to speak to his own mother.

So, which was it? How did he really feel about the mom he so often bragged about? Did he love the woman, or hate her guts? George's relationship with women in general followed much the same template. On the surface he was usually as nice as can be. And even seemed to encourage and build up his female protégés.

For troubled young women with low self-esteem, George could very well have seemed like a Godsend. As encouraging and supportive as he was on the surface however, no one knew of the dark undercurrent of animosity that flowed through him.

No one knew of course—until it was too late.

Bouncing from One Place to Another

Perhaps it's an understatement, but George Russell Jr. was not the type of person that could be figured out very easily. He was the scion of a well-to-do upper middle-class family, and hung out with upper middle-class people. Even when he was unemployed and homeless, he still very much considered himself a part of the upper crust.

He was soon back on the prowl on Mercer Island, crashing with friends, and breaking into other places when friends weren't quite so generous. It was the latter methodology of breaking and entering that would become an increasingly worrying trend as it pertained to George.

Another trend was that he was losing his ability to coerce his young friends into going along with his plans. This was especially true for his *female friends.* George had reached a point where girls his age didn't want anything to do with him. More mature women his age were usually pursuing a degree, a career, and expected any prospective man in their life to be doing the same.

Yet here was George now well into his 20s with nothing much to show for his time on planet Earth but the latest hangover. On a bad day, he was too old and washed up to even impress young and impressionable teens. Stinging from the rejection of multiple women, it seems that George began to quietly plot out how he would take his vengeance out on the female population as a whole. It could be said that this was the moment in which George Russell Jr. crossed a point of no return.

George's growing misogyny coincided with his growing interest in breaking into homes. It wasn't long before things got ugly. For it was a short time later that George escalated his crimes, and went from breaking and entering, to confinement, to outright assault. Immediately before his rampage however, George briefly tried his luck once again at the straight life.

He got a job at a local video game arcade. He managed to save up his money for a while, and soon he was the proud owner of a used car. The car was soon wrecked however, and George was also soon caught breaking the law. He had embezzled some $23,000 from the arcade. It's a wonder that charges were not filed, but George was of course promptly fired from the job.

He was now pushing 30, and roving the streets with abandon. No longer the loveable house guest of his youth, he was sleeping wherever he could. As fashionable as his pretensions might have been, much of the time he was crashing in nothing better than a garbage dumpster. It was around this time that a young woman by the name of Tami Smith was introduced to George by way of a mutual friend, Mike Weisenburgh.

Tami and Mike were down at the local Denny's restaurant, which was a popular hang-out of George's at the time. George could be seen taking up space at

Denny's just about all hours of the day. Tami and Mike walked in and George immediately made a beeline for Mike, shook his hand, and began talking his game. George came on really strong, but in an easygoing way that immediately put Tami at ease.

And despite any misgivings, she began to fall for him. George had become a regular fixture amongst her and Mike's mutual circle of friends, and it wasn't uncommon to find him at a friend's house cooking himself (and whoever might want some) a heaping portion of spaghetti. Tami however, soon became aware of George's criminal tendencies. Shortly after they met, he landed himself in jail and called her, begging that she make a character witness statement to police. He wanted her to vouch that he was her roommate and that he had a steady job.

Tami didn't quite get it—but she figured if it helped George—she would do it. Police later called her home, and she told them everything George had expected her to say. The cops seemed satisfied enough, after she vouched for him, and let her know that George would be released shortly.

According to Tami, she and George became the best of friends, staying out late and drinking together. During this period, George also met a girl named Mindy, whom he encountered at a nightclub called the Black Angus. Mindy soon became another prospective target for George, and he would crash at the homes of young women such as she and Tami's homes, as a means of survival. Without them, he would indeed have been homeless.

It was in order to partially pay for his room and board, and bankroll his partying, that George became a cat burglar, slipping into houses and stealing valuables which he could later cash in. The relationship between the roommates deteriorated over the next few months however, and after an eviction notice was served and a row over how to make up back rent erupted, a terrible argument ensued.

Mindy told George to leave for good. He did—but not before destroying just about *all* of her property. After he left, Mindy managed to get a restraining order against him, but he still periodically snuck around the property, and even broke into her car on more than one occasion. George in the meantime, had become a regular at the aforementioned nightclub—Black Angus—until he ran afoul of a cocktail waitress known as "G.B. Coffin."

She told the bouncers that he was bothering her, and they bounced him right out of the club. George Russell Jr. was heard making some rather ominous threats as he left however, including a threat to kill that pesky cocktail waitress that had him tossed out.

It wouldn't be long before some of his threats would become reality.

Half-Truths Flavored with Plenty of Lies

George had been known to the police for many years, but for most of that time he was viewed as a harmless delinquent. He was a guy that was in and out of jail for petty crimes, but besides these minor infractions he never did anything very serious. The situation began to change in May of 1990, when much more ominous reports of break-ins were being reported in Mercer Island.

It seemed that someone was prepping themselves to become a serious predator. Police were soon on the lookout for a man who was seen coming in and out of houses late at night. That man fit the profile of George Russell Jr. Police Officer Cecilia Doucet ran into George first hand on a routine patrol. She didn't know him at the time, but he had been aggressively squealing the tires of a Chevy Capri station wagon.

She stopped the car and spoke to George, who was behind the wheel. Even though he didn't even have a driver's license on his person, George was as congenial as can be. He ended up just getting a warning, but Officer Cecilia was sure to make a mental note of the strange character she had pulled over, because something about him just seemed *off*.

It was a short time later that another officer happened to have a run-in with George. There seemed to be some sort of altercation downtown where a crowd of people had gathered. The police rolled up and a man fitting George's description was seen getting into a car with a younger guy. The patrol officer approached and asked if everything was all right.

George then proceeded to lie through his teeth claiming that the other people involved were giving his young friend a hard time. But George was sure to insist that everything was all right now and thanked the officer for showing up. Unsure of what else to do, the officer waved the car on, and George left.

The cop then spoke to the other party however, and learned that George had been doing more than just breaking up a fight. George had been impersonating a police officer. During the course of his half-baked impersonation, he had waved a gun, and had even struck one of them with it. This was a serious offense.

Realizing as much, the cop got on his radio and put out an all-points bulletin to nab George, the impersonator, before he caused any further damage. George was tracked down a short time later, and ended up leading police on a brief high-speed chase. The chase ended when George crashed into a construction site.

Once the car came to a stop, he hopped out of the car with hands raised, apparently ready to surrender. Ever-cognizant of the crimes he could be charged with, and always intent to minimize them as much as possible—George by this point, had tossed the gun aside.

It was after speaking with the guy that was with George that night—a young kid named Mitchell, that police really got an earful. The young man claimed that he had indeed been on the losing end of a fight when George showed up and "rescued" him. He then agreed to go with George, since he didn't want to stick around where all of his antagonists were prowling about.

Here we see that George, despite all of his deviousness, may very well have been doing his best to save a young man who was being bullied and picked on by a bunch of tough guys on the street. It's just too bad that during the process of doing all of this, he was committing a whole slew of criminal offenses, such as impersonating a police officer, hitting folks upside the head with guns, and leading (real) police on a dangerous high-speed chase.

But yes, this was the complicated, convoluted life that George lived. And one can't forget, that even his seemingly virtuous act of coming to this young man's rescue, was likely the first step toward him ingratiating himself with the youngster, so that he could control him and use him for his own purposes later on. For that was indeed what George was in the habit of doing.

He found ways to present himself as the good guy, so that he could crash at someone's house, borrow money, borrow cars, whatever the case may be. This was the strategy he had developed in life, just to get by. A short time later he played the same tactic on another young man—Smith McClain.

He borrowed Smith's truck in fact, on the night of his first murder. For it was in late June, that he took the truck and used it to transport the dead body of a woman he had murdered—Mary Anne Pohlreich. Ms.

Pohlreich's corpse was then discovered in a dumpster behind the parking lot of the Black Angus nightclub/restaurant in Bellevue, on June 23rd, 1990.

One of the first cops alerted to the scene was police Detective Marvin Skeen. He had heard the alarm raised over his radio, as the developing crime scene was described, "a male body naked, possible DOA. Behind the Black Angus restaurant." Officer Skeen quickly made his way over to the scene of the crime to see what he could do to help.

It was upon his arrival, that he realized that the radio announcement was wrong—it wasn't a *male*—the body belonged to a young woman. He described the girl as being five foot eight, and perhaps 150 pounds, with reddish brown hair. Completely nude, the young lady was obviously put into a posed position by her killer. She lay flat on her back, with both her legs and arms crossed.

Her head was slightly turned to the left, and oddly, a lid to a spent Frito lay chip dip container was covering one of her eyes. She had been murdered, considering the state of the body, she had many bruises and abrasions, including a nasty head wound. What had happened to her?

Smith McClain, in the meantime, finally had his truck returned to him and was shocked to find that it smelled horrible inside the cab of the vehicle. The Toyota pickup truck was his pride and joy and he had always tried his best to keep it in pristine condition. Now, thanks to George, it contained a revolting smell.

Smith assumed someone must have thrown up in the vehicle, the very thought of which sent him into a tailspin of depression. If anyone has ever had someone throw up in their car, they would sympathize with how this guy felt. Vomit immediately leaves a lasting stink in a vehicle, and is very hard to clean up. With a liberal dose of baking soda to absorb the noxious particles, and a lot of good old-fashioned scrubbing, one might be able to get rid of it. If the sick person happened to puke inside the vents of the vehicle, you might as well forget it.

As it pertains to Smith's truck, it was indeed just about as bad as described. Or maybe even worse. Because the more Smith struggled to clean up the mess, the more he thought that whatever it was—it didn't smell like vomit, but something even *more* vile. He hunted in his spare time, and as he scrubbed away at the floorboards of his truck, his mind went back to when he once gutted a deer.

As the innards of the deer spilled out, that strong smell was similar to what he was experiencing in the truck. *What the hell did George do last night?* Those were the kind of thoughts that likely came to Smith McClain's mind, as he struggled to rid his Toyota pickup truck of the terrible after-aroma that lingered.

George eventually called him, and told him a rambling story about how he had picked up a woman from the bar, but after a while realized he had too much to drink. According to George, he realized it too late— and suddenly threw up his booze along with a smelly portion of clam chowder he had just eaten. According to George this was the cause of the stench in the pickup truck. Upon hearing all of this, Smith was outraged—not only was he annoyed that George so flippantly admitted to destroying his truck, but also by the fact that he could tell that George was *lying.*

George was good at telling stories, and when with more gullible people, he still had a chance of being able to get folks to believe what he told them. But Smith on the other hand, had a powerful bullshit detector, and he knew when someone was feeding him a line of bull or not. To him, George's story sounded ridiculous and absurd, and he called him out on it. For one thing, Smith had never known George to "drink too much."

Smith had seen him drink like a fish on many occasions, and typically was none the worse for wear. Smith had *never* seen him drink so much that he threw up. Smith also knew George well enough by now, to understand that he was a habitual liar and constantly told untruths either to cover his tracks, or simply because he liked embellishing, exaggerating, and lying.

Yes, lying was just what George did. Now Smith had to wonder just which parts of George's half-truths were flavored with his over the top, outrageous lies.

Throwing Them Off His Trail

As the search for the killer of Mary Anne Pohlreich progressed, her autopsy was revealing some rather shocking details about the manner in which she had died. Although at first glance, she did not appear to be badly beaten, the internal injuries she suffered told another story. Her liver had been split in half. This apparently occurred right after she had been kicked so hard, that her own spine sliced into her internal organs.

She also had some pretty serious skull fractures indicating that she had suffered blunt force trauma to the head. Even more distressing, there was evidence that some sort of object had been shoved into her rearend, causing severe damage, that ripped through her anus.

There was also some indication that the same treatment had been given to her vagina, which was also torn and savaged by penetration. And not all of this penetration was done with a foreign object, since identifiable sperm was discovered inside the victim.

Along with all of this terrible brutality, it was also clear that she had been repeatedly struck across the face by whoever had so savagely attacked her. Even so, the actual identity of the victim—let alone her killer—had yet to be identified. It was Mary Anne's roommate, Theresa Veary, who first sounded the alarm that the murdered woman found outside the Black Angus just might be Mary Anne Pohlreich.

For Theresa knew Mary to be a punctual and responsible roommate, and when she didn't return home one evening as planned, Theresa immediately sensed that something was wrong. Theresa herself had just returned from a camping trip, and fully expected Mary to be home by the time she arrived. Instead, she was greeted by a blaring alarm clock and a house full of hungry cats.

The alarm clock was blaring because Mary wasn't there that morning like she usually was to turn it off. As for the cats, the couple of cats the roommates had in their home, were usually fed in the morning, but since no one had been home, they were left meowing with their stomachs growling. Theresa reported Mary's absence to police and soon enough it was determined that the dead body they had picked up belonged to the missing woman.

Along with helping the police identify the victim, Theresa also provided some crucial personal information about her. Theresa informed police that Mary was known as something of a tease at the clubs she frequented. According to roommate Theresa, the 27-year-old Mary would go to bars and casually flirt with guys enough to get them to buy her drinks all night, only to then abruptly ditch them and go home.

Although there are some pretty obvious dangers in leading on angry drunks in such a manner, Mary Anne was apparently never too concerned about it. She was ready to tell off anyone who gave her a hard time, or in some instances, she simply laughed in their face. Mary Anne apparently never imagined that someone would actually get violent with her—but that is most certainly what happened when she tried this routine with George Russell Jr.

Further inquiries found eyewitnesses who had encountered Mary Anne at the Black Angus before her murder. She had been pretty drunk and had been trying her flirtatious routine on several men who were present. The disc jockey in particular, remembered her, and recalled that he was annoyed because she came up to him several times requesting that he play M. C. Hammer's, "You Can't Touch This" which was a hit at the time.

It was a week after the murder meanwhile, on June 30th, of 1990, that George Russell Jr. made a return to the nightclub scene. The local clubs were now crawling with undercover police officers. George was able to easily spot them out, and rather than hide from them, in typical George fashion, he sauntered right over. He started light-hearted conversations, and even offered tips.

At first the cops assigned to the case, thought the George was an unexpected aid to this difficult investigation, but they soon realized that he was feeding them a whole lot of misinformation. Even worse, according to one officer—Earl Barnes— George actually seemed to be trying to get information *from them.* He began to ask questions about how far along they were in the investigation, and what kind of clues they had found.

In retrospect it would seem that George was checking in with the cops to see how close they were to his own trail. Shortly thereafter, George meanwhile, popped up at his old roommate Mindy's place. Despite the restraining order against him, he cheerfully strode in, accompanied by two young girls. Mindy was stunned, but since George seemed friendly, she wasn't willing to create a confrontation and make him angry.

Instead, she quietly listened while he informed her that he was just there to pick up his cat. George had a calico cat named Sasha that he never bothered to retrieve after his falling out with Mindy. Yet despite the fact that Mindy was the one who had cared for the animal up until this point, he was now there to collect. She readily gave the cat over to George, and he then handed it to one of the women he was with. Mindy overheard George telling his new female friend that the cat was a "gift."

Perhaps George had run out of stolen rings and necklaces to hand out, when he alighted upon the notion that he could retrieve his long-lost cat and offer it up as a present. Mindy watched as the strange group filed out of her apartment, simply glad that they had left without further incident.

George was actually up to his old tricks, and soon he was living with yet another set of young women. He had met them at Denny's and they were cautious with him at first. But once they realized that he ran in a lot of the same social circles, they let their guard down and the next thing they knew, he moved right in.

At first, they were quite enamored with the guy. He presented himself as a good friend, and even a protector. The girls liked to throw parties and there was more than one occasion in which he gave a rowdy guy the boot. If anyone got a little too frisky with his female roommates, George stood up for them and laid down the law. Things became a little strange however, when George began telling his roomies that he was an undercover cop.

Not only that—he told them that he was working on the murder case of Mary Anne Pohlreich. Soon however, folks would come to realize that he wasn't trying to *find* Mary's killer—*he was the killer.*

George kept up his game of playing detective and one evening he even brought a couple of real detectives in—police Detective Earl Barnes and Jeff Gomes. The girls were really impressed by this. So much so, that they hid their marijuana, and seemed to think they were about to be busted. They only calmed down, when the detectives assured them that they were "not here for that."

The girls were then shocked to learn the real reason behind the intrusion. The police wanted to know more about a mutual friend of theirs named Damien Middleton. The cops seemed to think that he somehow had something to do with Mary Anne's murder. And pretty soon they knew why—because that's what George had told them.

Yes, George was trying to frame their buddy Damien for murder. Damien as it turns out, was the last steady boyfriend Mary Anne Pohlreich had. Unfortunately for Damien, this lead did appeal to the detectives, because murders are indeed often committed by those who were closest to the victims.

But even without suspecting George, the young women knew that Damien couldn't have been the killer. He was the nicest, sweetest guy they knew. So why was George so insistent on leading the cops to him?

Just to get them off of his trail of course.

The Killer Strikes Again

The next murder victim of George Russell Jr. was a 35-year-old woman by the name of Carol Beethe, who turned up dead on August 9th, of 1990. Carol's corpse had been discovered by her young daughter, Kelly. Kelly was only 13 years old at the time, and she was obviously shocked and horrified. In her stunned state however, she did manage to call her father.

It was Carol's ex-husband Mr. Paul Beethe, who after taking just a brief glimpse into the room, somehow determined that the whole thing was a suicide. This led to much confusion later on—since even a rookie cop, after one glance at this mess, was likely to realize that there was *no way* that such a grisly scene was self-inflicted.

Just as had been the case with Mary Anne Pohlreich, the dead body had been placed in a grotesquely staged pose. But whereas Mary Anne's legs had been crossed, the bare legs of Carol Beethe were wide open, as her nude form lay sprawled out on her bed. Even worse, in between those bare legs had been placed the barrel of a shotgun.

Was this why the murder has initially been dubbed a suicide by her ex-husband? Did he actually think that she used her toes to pull the trigger and just naturally fell back in this position?

As mentioned, closer inspection would quickly rule any such notion out. As the investigation began, the police questioned Carol's two daughters, Kelly and

Jamie. Kelly was 13, and Jamie was only 9 years old at the time.

Little Jamie understandably enough, was crying the whole time, and not much could be learned from her. Older sister Kelly, proved to be much more open to questioning, and she soon became a big help to investigators. It was Kelly who clued cops in to all that had transpired before the incident occurred. To say that Kelly's testimony was helpful would be an understatement—it turns out, she just might have been an eyewitness.

For according to her account, she woke up around 4:30 that morning to hear a sound in the hallway. She looked out from her door, and thought she saw the shadowy form of a man walking down the hall, shining a flashlight. Although this probably should have been alarming—and likely would have been to someone a little older—Kelly claimed that she rationalized the whole thing by figuring that it was probably her mom's recent boyfriend, "Tom Jones" who occasionally stayed over.

It would be learned that her mother frequently had her boyfriends stay overnight, and so the girls had come to expect these sorts of intrusions. And so it was, that Kelly thought the visitor was just mom's boyfriend, Tom Jones, paying a nocturnal visit. Even so, she was sure to look outside her window to make sure that she could see the familiar sight of Tom's Corvette parked outside.

She didn't see it however, and soon fell fast asleep. She then woke up a few hours later to find the terrible sight of her mother's dead body. In retrospect it's a bit hard to fathom how Kelly—or anyone else—could have slept through what must have been a truly horrific encounter.

It's unclear how George might have kept Carol from screaming, or otherwise minimized the sounds of the struggle, but it would later be determined that Carol did indeed fight for her life. Having said that, there should have been crashing and banging, and all manner of distressing sounds coming from her bedroom.

Considering that Kelly seemed to black out and fall asleep right before this melee ensued, almost makes one wonder if her mind somehow blanked out the memories altogether. Perhaps she did hear something, but in her frightened state simply put the blanket over her head and pretended that this particular startling brand of bogeyman—George Russell Jr.—wasn't there. Maybe she successfully blocked the whole thing from her mind. This was, however, all that Kelly consciously remembered at the time that the police questioned her.

During the course of the investigation, detectives would learn that the victim—Carol Beethe—was a local cocktail waitress. She was a popular and attractive, 36-year-old woman, who was known for her tiny, petite figure. Carol, in fact, barely reached five feet tall, and barely weighed 100 pounds on the scale. With her long curly main trailing her trim figure, she was definitely eye-catching.

Unfortunately, she must have caught the wrong set of eyes on the night that she was murdered. The autopsy would show that she had been savagely beaten as well as violated, post-mortem, with a shot gun and perhaps even other random objects. It would be determined that the gun itself had been inserted some five and a half inches deep into her vagina.

It was also known at this point that the gun belonged to Carol Beethe herself. The killer had simply made use of it, in his staging of his victim. As investigators probed deeper into Carol's personal life in the meantime, it soon became clear that she was no stranger to wild affairs. Along with the string of boyfriends, it´s said that she was fairly promiscuous.

One person who knew her in fact, went so far as to claim that she had been sexually involved with eight different men over the course of just a few years. Even so, boyfriend Tom Jones was the closest thing to a steady lover that Carol had. Police learned that the relationship was rocky to say the least. They both cheated on each other, but for some reason, although Carol thought nothing of cheating on Tom, she became irate when she learned that he was cheating on her.

Police learned of one outrageous instance in which Carol and another woman that Tom was seeing, discovered that they were both having sex with Tom. The two women decided to get back at him, by sending a bouquet of "black roses" to his job site. The roses allegedly included a card with a bunch of nude rear ends emblazoned on the front, with the message, "You're the biggest asshole of all."

Besides exchanging such over-the-top insults, the couple were said to get into routine arguments, some of them rather explosive. Tom himself had been previously arrested for domestic assault in the past. All of this of course, made Tom a leading suspect in this murder case in the eyes of police.

Soon enough, Tom was brought into questioning. Tom was of course, highly upset. It's said that he was hyperventilating during the police interrogation. It's perfectly understandable of course for someone to become a nervous wreck when they realize not only is their girlfriend dead, but they are being wrongly accused of the murder. But in the eyes of his interrogators, the nerves were not over fears of being railroaded for a crime he did not commit—but the guilty agitation of one who has been found out.

The fact that Tom stated offhand, that he occasionally "blacked out" and didn't remember things he had done—certainly didn't help him either. Tom also refused to take a polygraph (lie detector test) which was deemed suspicious.

George in the meantime, had made a return to the young women—Bobbie DeGroot, Suzy Jetley, Sara Amundson, and Jenny Graves—who had previously put him up. He put on the charm and soon was drinking with them, and even making them dinner. George among other things, was apparently a good cook and they appreciated the home cooked meals.

It was during one of these "wholesome" get-togethers with George, that he supposedly began making remarks about the two murdered women Mary Anne Pohlreich and Carole Beethe. He disparaged detectives and claimed that they were "stupid" for not seeing the connection between the two cases. Pressed further, George insisted that the women matched an exact same profile, in age (their ages were actually different) appearance, and lifestyle.

George Russell Jr. claimed that any good detective would realize that the same killer must have killed these two women. Even so, at this point in the investigation, George was apparently the only one who felt that way. Yes, while police were still looking into Tom Jones for the slaying of Carol, and coming up entirely blank as it pertained to the murder of Mary Anne—George was dropping hints left and right.

Police in the meantime, had managed to track down Damien whom George had previously attempted to frame for the murder of Mary Anne Pohlreich. Damien, when questioned by police, appeared genuinely shocked.

He apparently didn't even know that Mary Anne was killed. Police took some hair and saliva samples from him, which subsequently failed to return any hits. Previously railroaded Damien appeared to have been cleared from the list of suspects.

George. in the meantime, would strike again, killing Andrea (better known as Randi) Levine in her own bed on August 31st, of 1990. Randi was home alone when George apparently broke in and found her sleeping. He made short work of her—and her dead body was discovered a few days later.

It was on the morning of September 3rd, that Randi Levine's landlord phoned 911 to report that she had been discovered dead in the basement apartment that she rented from them. She rented the apartment from a married couple, Bob and Patty Hays, who lived right upstairs from her.

Randi and her loved ones likely felt that this sort of arrangement was a very protective one. Randi had a nice older couple, situated just above her basement apartment, to look after her. They likely never realized that cat burglar-turned-serial killer George Russell Jr. would sneak into that basement without anyone being the wiser.

It was Patty who realized something was wrong when she observed that Randi's two cats were meowing, apparently hungry and unfed. It wasn't like Randi not to feed her cats. This led her to go down into the basement to check on Randi herself. She found Randi dead in her bed, with blood splattered everywhere. She ran to her husband Bob in a panic and he contacted emergency services.

Investigators on the scene of the murder were in for a gruesome sight. Like the other victims, the killer had placed her dead body in a gruesome pose. She was nude, placed flat on her back with her legs spread wide open. A self-help book on sexual intimacy called *More Joy of Sex* had been sinisterly put under left arm, to make it look as if she had been reading it.

Her right arm in the meantime was languorously stretched out, as if she were resting comfortably. But her tortured corpse was by no means at rest. Her head had been battered in so bad, it's said that bits of her brain were actually dripping out the side of it. Her mouth had a vibrator, cruelly popped into it—likely as a last-minute act of macabre malice.

There were stab wounds all over her body and her right breast even bore slices that seemed to represent a twisted game of tic-tac-toe. It was a shocking sight, but the investigators had to ignore their disgust and do their work. Evidence was collected, photos were taken, and the hunt for—what was now a serial killer at work—had begun.

Hunt for a Serial Killer

In the aftermath of Randi's killing—just as was the case in the aftermath of the slayings of the other two women—the leads were scarce. But they were not non-existent. Shortly before her death, Randi had actually complained that she thought she had seen someone prowling around. Bob Hays the landlord, took the complaint seriously enough to install some motion detectors on the property.

Unfortunately, such things did not serve as any sort of a deterrent for the killer. Investigators believed that the intruder had actually slipped in through a garage door that was up just a crack for the cats to crawl under. Unfortunately, along with the cats, it also let in a cat burglar—skinny old George. One thing of interest that popped up during the course of the investigation into Randi's murder was the fact that her prized amethyst ring was missing.

A friend of hers when going through her belongings, made a comment to that effect, and this set off an alert to look out for the missing ring. It was clear that the killer must have taken it. It was hoped that the search for the ring therefore, would lead to the killer. The most obvious way to connect a stolen item to a criminal would be for them to pawn it. The pawnshop would have records—even fingerprints of the person.

If he had done something like that, the ring and therefore the crime would have been easily traced back to George Russell Jr. But George had a slippery way with rings, and it wasn't long before he slipped it onto the finger of a female friend of his, a young woman by the name of Dacia Jubinville.

Investigators were becoming more and more convinced in the meantime, that all three of the recent killings were the work of the same person. The staging of a corpse in a macabre pose is unusual. It's not usually done in most murders. The fact that this same feat had been repeated three times in a row, seemed to indicate a connection. The police did not want to cause a panic by announcing to the press that they likely had a serial killer in their midst, but they had begun to quietly remark among themselves that this was probably the case.

It was around this time that those who knew George began to consider him as a suspect. The police that knew him long ago considered all of his recent run-ins with the law and behavior and considered him a likely contender for murder. It was around this time that a cop working the beat on the night that the first victim was killed, outside the Black Angus, recalled George leaving with an obviously intoxicated woman.

He also recalled a man complaining that his truck was missing. The truck, if recovered, would perhaps provide enough clues to break this case wide open. As such, the hunt for the truck began in earnest. Now that they had their suspect, they could only wonder when he might strike next. Well—that fateful moment occurred on September 9th, of 1990.

For it was on this fateful day that George attacked (and likely would have killed) a 16-year-old girl named Nicole DeVita. Nicole had been visiting some friends who lived near her parents' place, when she decided

50

to walk back to her parents' house in the early morning hours. By the time she got back to her parents' place however, she found that the door was locked.

She tried to alert her brother Tony by throwing rocks at his window. It was while she was calling out Tony's name that George stepped out of the darkness and pretended to be a familiar face. He didn't really know Tony, but since he had heard the girl calling his name, he was crafty enough to take advantage. George readily proclaimed that he and Tony were the best of friends. Not only that—he would help her get a hold of him.

It was while she had her back turned, and was still trying to find a way inside her family home, that George ambushed her. He knocked her to the ground and began hitting with a large rock he had picked up off the ground. Fortunately, her screams finally alerted her family, and even as she was being pummeled into unconsciousness, they managed to come out in time to drive her assailant away.

She later woke up in the hospital, and was able to give a fairly good account of what had happened to her. She described him as an African American male, in his late 20s (George was actually 32), and stated that he was around five feet nine and had a skinny, wiry frame. It was a generalized description, but considering the crime, George's MO, and the fact that the incident occurred right in his backyard, he was immediately of interest.

George Russell Jr., in the meantime was soon picked up for an outstanding warrant. The arrest occurred on

September 12th. This arrest was just one of many in his life, and he likely figured he would soon be back out on the streets in no time. He always was in the past—so why should anything be different this time around?

But although the warrant he was arrested for had nothing to do with the murders, he was now a *prime* suspect. As such, the police were eager to find a means to link him to the crime before George found his way out of those revolving jail doors once again. So it was that that the questioning began.

As was typically the case, George was as cool as a cucumber and was more than ready to speak in complete half-truths. The detectives got him to admit that he knew victims Randi and Mary, but beyond saying that they were general acquaintances, he was not willing to say that he knew them very well. As for Carol Beethe? He refused to have ever known her at all.

So he claimed to have no knowledge of Carol. Nevertheless, the fact that he acknowledged knowing the other two murder victims opened the door a crack. And now that this door had been cracked, the detectives were determined to pry it open the rest of the way. They continued to relentlessly question George on the matter, and eventually he started rambling about how he had once helped Randi Levine when her vehicle had broken down on the side of the road.

George, of course, was doing everything he could to paint himself in the best possible light. He was a good Samaritan helping a stranger who was in need. It could very well be that this story was true—George was known to help people on occasion. But usually, he did these things in order to get his marks to drop their defenses, and allow him to worm his way into their lives.

Yes, he very well could have introduced himself by way of a good deed, but it typically wasn't long before his intentions turned sinister. Yes, whether those intentions were to lie, manipulate, steal, attack, or kill—usually the very first deed of kindness, was just the icing on his sinister, sociopathic cake.

According to George, it was shortly after this incident, that he happened to run into Randi Levine at a party being held at a local club—Papagayo's. He also ended up admitting that he had stopped by her apartment on at least one occasion. As much as George liked to fabricate things, the more he talked, the more certain connections were made.

George had now gone from saying that Randi was just a random acquaintance, to stating that he had actually been over to her home. It wasn't long however, before he began throwing some of his so-called friends under the bus. And more convenient, self-serving half-truths and deceptions were in order.

He soon recalled an incident in which his old buddy Michael Weisenburgh, was arguing with another guy over who would take Randi home. George was talkative enough, but it was when the police asked if they could take some blood, saliva, and hair samples that George's demeanor changed.

At this point, he must have known he was in serious trouble, since he immediately insisted that he was done talking, and he wanted to speak to his lawyer. George was certainly not a novice, and he had interacted with police enough already in his life to know the drill. He knew that he didn't have to talk if he didn't want to—so it was at this crucial moment that he decided to plead the fifth.

That first fateful interrogation session of George Russell Jr. ended with him wanting to speak to an attorney. For most down and out criminal defendants, this likely would have meant them being given a low budget public defender assigned by the state. George Russell Jr. however, as estranged as he was from his former parents, had resources that most others did not.

For it was rich stepdad dentist, Dr. Wonzel Mobley and his ex-wife—George's mother Joyce—who stepped in to pick up the tab. Both of these high rollers had money to burn. Wonzel from his successful practice in dentistry and Joyce from her high paid salary as a college professor. Even though they had long been estranged from their son, they decided to finance his defense as best they could, resulting in him getting one of the best defense attorneys that money could buy.

Investigators were working overtime to try and link George to the killings, and would soon happen upon another major breakthrough. They combed through George's previous contacts and came upon a woman by the name of Dacia Jubinville. They spoke to her about George, just as they interviewed all of his acquaintances. And she happened to mention that

George on one occasion had given her a ring—a purple amethyst, to be exact.

This immediately got investigators´ attention, because they were well aware that Randi's distinct purple amethyst ring had been missing from the crime scene. They asked her what she had done with the ring and it was discovered that she had given it to a friend named David Vice. It was then learned that Vice had pawned it. Vice had actually hitchhiked with his girlfriend all the way down to Key West, when the guy, finding himself completely broke, remembered the ring—and decided to cash in.

Although George himself had not pawned it—this was the next best thing. For if police could link the pawn shop records to David Vice, and then to Dacia, and then in turn link Dacia to George, they have a working chain of evidence that George had stolen the ring from Randi. And since the ring went missing the night she was killed, that was more than enough circumstantial evidence to link George to the murder itself.

There was also the testimony of the lone survivor of Geroge's rampage—Nicole DeVita. Ms. DeVita could very well have been George's fourth murder, but her alert family had thwarted the attempt on her life. Even so, she didn't survive unphased. She had taken some truly nasty blows to the head, and even her memory of what had happened to her was faulty as a result.

She could provide some details of her assailant, and the details she provided generally lined up with George Russell Jr.'s profile, but due to the gaps in her own memory, not all of what she had to say was reliable. There was a question of what would even be admissible in court, after it was all said and done.

Nicole did however, provide one crucial and unexpected lead. She mentioned that George was friends with a local comic by the name of Steve Crandall. Investigators tracked down Crandall to learn more. Steve was quiet at first, but later he would relate that he had just heard that George had beaten his good friend Nicole, and that was enough to get him to want to talk. And soon it was clear, that George could plead the fifth as much as he wanted, but the details of his life and crimes would steadily emerge— regardless.

The Trial of George Russell Jr.

Interestingly enough, as prosecutors prepared to take the case against George Russell Jr. to trial, they signaled in advance that they wouldn't be seeking the death penalty. Instead, they were willing to settle for just life in prison. It's said that they did this in order to not "upset their strategy" as it pertained to keeping an even keel as it pertained to all three murders.

For the death penalty, crimes have to meet a high bar of both irrefutable evidence and clear cruelty. George may have clearly demonstrated the latter, but since much of the evidence across all three cases was circumstantial, the prosecution didn't want to risk missing that high bar for the death penalty, so instead they settled for just life in prison as a maximum possible sentence.

It was after this was decided, that the pre-trial hearings convened on August 2nd of 1991. During the hearing some of the most vigorous debate between the two sides was over whether or not there had been a significant degree of staging involved with each of the victims. At first glance, it might have seemed that the staging was obvious, but the factors involved were finessed by the defense to call into question some of the staging that occurred.

The first victim for example, was lying on her back with her arms crossed. It was suggested that perhaps the arms just fell into that position naturally when she

57

was being dragged. Those who carried this line of argument however, had a hard time explaining how it was she ended up with a fir cone in her hand. Was that an accident too? These were the kinds of debates that went back and forth during the hearing.

As the actual trial started, the witnesses were brought forward and the defense tried their best to cross examine them. One of the star witnesses for the prosecution turned out to be down-on-his-luck comic—Steve Crandall. Mr. Crandall was questioned and from the very beginning, he was made out to be some sort of antagonist of George, who was trying to pin the killings on him, out of spite.

At one point he was even asked point blank, "The reason you're here today is because you want to see Mr. Russell convicted—is that fair enough?" Steve Crandall wasn't going to fall for it however, and he was quick to set the questioner straight. He immediately shot back, "It's not fair enough. I'm here to testify that [George] tried to sell me a ring."

In other words, he wasn't there to either condemn or exonerate Geroge. He was just there to state the facts, of the little bit he knew. He knew that George had tried to sell him a ring. The cops said that ring belonged to a dead person—that's all he knew about it. Nothing more. Nothing less. End of story.

The defense, in the meantime, began to argue heavily that the state prosecution had the wrong person in court. They suggested that others, such as estranged boyfriend of victim number 1—Tom Jones, and estranged ex-husband of victim number 2—Paul Beethe, were also likely suspects. Alongside all of this of course, was the argument that none of these killings were connected.

The defense relentlessly tried to blow holes in the theory that there was only one man (presumably George Russell Jr.) behind the murders. The prosecution however, presented an FBI witness to vouch for the likelihood that just one killer was involved. Russell, in the meantime, sat through all of this, typically decked out in a designer suit (likely furnished by his rich stepdad).

He was fairly detached throughout these proceedings, seen either daydreaming or reading a book. On some occasions however, he appeared to be taking some rather spurious notes—as if he himself were part of the legal team, figuring out what the next best move would be.

Some of the most damning testimony in the meantime, came from the four young women he had briefly roomed with prior to the murders. Interestingly, their testimony was both flattering as well as damning.

For while the girls might have gushed about how he was a nice, intelligent guy with whom they genuinely enjoyed spending time—several off-hand anecdotes would have struck anyone as being fairly *alarming*.

It was remarked for example, that George often spoke of murder cases, and in particular had been following the case of Mary Ann Pohlreich fairly closely. It was also revealed that he carried a police scanner, and often left the house in dark clothes at night. The girls naively insisted that he was on undercover police work. A quick check of the records of course, made clear the fact that George never worked for the police.

So, what was he doing with a police scanner, sneaking out of the house in dark clothes in the middle of the night? Most likely breaking into houses! So it was that the girls´ own naïve, glowing testimony about their hero George served to help shower further condemnation on the skinny shoulders of George Russell Jr.

More evidence would arrive in the meantime, by way of certain lab tests that had been carried out on the fabric of the fateful Toyota pickup truck that victim number one—Mary Anne Pohlreich, had died in. That truck that Geroge had borrowed from his good friend Smith McClain had now been thoroughly examined and the results were rather telling.

Yes, despite the fact that it had already been thoroughly cleaned by its owner, blood was found. The blood in the truck matched Mary Anne´s blood type. Even further links had been discovered with Randi in the meantime, since hair retrieved from George's gym bag proved to be a match with the hairs on her own head. George, it seemed, had taken some of Randi's bright red hair as a souvenir of sorts, and stashed it away in his bag.

As much as he often touted himself as being *smarter* than the police—this was a very *stupid* move on George's part. He either never thought that this handful of hair would be found, or he didn't realize that forensic science could link the strands of hair back to his victim.

It was just before the defense rested that the judge actually inquired with George directly to see if he would like to take the stand. Considering his narcissistic tendencies, one has to wonder why George didn't jump at the chance. The guy had spent his whole life trying to smooth-talk his way out of situations—so why not?

George however, likely under the strong recommendation of his attorneys, continued to plead the fifth. He wasn't talking. It was after George recommitted himself to silence in this manner that the defense rested and the prosecution commenced.

The state first demonstrated the depravity of the crimes, speaking of the beautiful women who lost their lives, and how terrible their final moments must have been. They also emphasized the various items that had linked Russell to the victims. Their efforts were effective. For after 22 hours of deliberation, the verdict rendered by the jurors in November 1991 was: guilty.

He was found guilty of first-degree murder in the death of Mary Anne Pohlreich. And he was found guilty of aggravated first-degree murder in the Carol Beethe and Randi Levine cases. It's said that he showed absolutely no emotion whatsoever when the verdict was read.

He was then sent off to Washington's Clallam Bay Corrections Center, for two life imprisonment terms plus 28 years, where he remains behind bars to this very day.

George Takes a Good Long Look at the Truth

George Russell Jr. was (and would still be) quite an unusual human specimen. But his most dangerous characteristics boiled down to the fact that he had great charisma—yet, like most sociopaths, he completely lacked a conscience. He could talk just about *anyone* into *anything*, and then have no remorse whatsoever over what might befall the other person. This was true as it pertained to using other people— either emotionally, physically, or financially.

He was prepared to use his smooth charm to get whatever he wanted out of people, and then equally prepared to leave them flat. In classic sociopathic fashion, he seemed to view himself as the *only* one with any feelings worth considering. The world was a great stage in which he was the *only* one who mattered, and everyone else were just props—just means to an end, and once that end was reached, everyone else was disposable.

Like most sociopaths George was also very smart. It's been said that he has a genius IQ. He was certainly smart enough to know what happened to those who transgressed the law. He knew the consequences of breaking the law from a legal perspective, even if he had no comprehension of it on a moral level. He may not have understood that others had feelings, but he understood that if he was caught hurting someone else, he could end up in jail.

So it was that George, while still not caring about how he used, abused, or harmed others, grew up with only the threat of legal repercussion holding him in check. One could wager that there may be more people out there than is first realized who fall into this kind of sociopathic category.

Perhaps they *pretend* to care for others—and to care for the rules of society. But in reality, it's only fear of legal repercussions (and perhaps even collective social scorn) which keeps them from acting out in the worst possible fashion. But the laws that our society hold up, to prevent outrageous behavior, only kept George in check for so long.

For it was that same genius IQ of his that had somehow convinced him that he was intelligent enough to outsmart the police, and the laws of civilized society that they enforced. Yes, George, trotting around with his police scanner, had become absolutely convinced that the laws no longer applied to him, since he could find his own ways around them.

He had learned how to slip in and out of houses undetected, and he figured he could probably kill without being detected as well. He had no concern or compassion for those he killed. And once he had convinced himself that he needn't even worry about legal repercussions—all bets were off. He considered himself one step ahead of law enforcement, and intended to remain one step ahead for as long as possible.

This was the deadly mix of callous sociopathic tendency, murderous aggression, and hubris, that created the perfect storm for serial-killing George

Russell Jr. He killed three people, and likely would have killed more if he hadn't been caught. Along with his direct victims, George during his rampage, affected the lives of countless others who either knew the victims or *knew him.*

Yes, one could make a good argument that it was the latter who were likely affected the most. For it was those who actually considered George Russell Jr. a "friend" who were probably the most blindsided by what happened. It is indeed hard to believe that someone who one comes to call "friend", whose company they generally enjoy, and whom one even might consider a "nice guy" could suddenly be revealed as a monstrous serial killer.

Such a revelation is so devastating, that it creates a situation where one might find it difficult to trust anyone. Scanning a crowd of pleasant, smiling faces—one is left wondering if any one of those happy, nice people could be a killer—a killer just like George.

Interestingly, one red flag that stood out to some friends of George Russell Jr. was the fact that George seemed to be fascinated with the likes of serial killer, Ted Bundy. The wretched Ted Bundy, of course, was yet another guy—known for being charismatic and charming, just like George—yet also just as much a terrible killer.

Did George Russell Jr. have some sort of affinity with Bundy because, deep down, he knew they suffered from the same defects in their personality? Bundy had become a sociopathic monster who had—either *never* had—or had somehow *lost* all connection to any

65

sense of compassion, or remorse. It was these terrible personal defects that allowed Bundy to kill, and then go about his everyday life like nothing had happened.

Perhaps in his few moments of clarity as he stared in the mirror, George too knew that something about himself was terribly *off* when compared to other people.

Perhaps even today, in 2023, in his jail cell, after he's run through his daily rehearsal of lies and denials, something deep inside him is quietly acknowledging some small semblance of the truth.

The truth of just how extremely deranged and off kilter he really was.

Further Readings

Now that we've brought this book to a close, you will find here useful resources covering multiple aspects of this case. Feel free to go through them on your own.

Charmer: A Ladies' Man and His Victims. Olsen, Jack
This book by seasoned true crime writer Jack Olsen provides a great overview of the life and crimes of Charles Russell Jr. This text follows the course of his life from childhood, to young adulthood, and ultimately to his rise as the most notorious killer of Mercer Island.

Signature Killers. Keppel, Robert
This is a classic true crime book that goes over George's case as well as many others that fit a similar profile. The book takes a look at killers who leave their own signature calling cards with their victims.

Made in the USA
Las Vegas, NV
01 December 2024